The
Missing Link

by
SYDNEY BANKS

The Missing Link

Distributed by:
In the US: In Canada:
Lone Pine Publishing   Canada Book Distributors - Booklogic
1808 B Street NW, Suite 140   11414-119 Street NW
Auburn, WA 98001   Edmonton, AB T5G 2X6
USA   Canada
1-800-518-3541   1-800-661-9017

Library and Archives Canada Cataloguing in Publication
Banks, Sydney, author
     The missing link / by Sydney Banks.
First published: Ganges, B.C. : International Human Relations
     Consultants, 1998.
ISBN 978-1-77213-017-1 (pbk)   ISBN 978-1-77213-011-9 (e-pub)
     1. Spiritualism (Philosophy). 2. Psychology and philosophy.
I. Title.
B841.B35 2016   129   C2016-903110-1

Senior Editor: Nancy Foulds
Production Manager: David Dodge
Layout & Production: Rob Weidemann
Book Design: Richard Mayer
Cover Design: Gregory Brown

PC: 33

Dedication

In admiration of the

many people throughout

the world who encounter

suffering every day and

try to alleviate it.

SYDNEY BANKS
Author, Philosopher
and Theosophist

———➤●◄———

Sydney Banks, a well-known author and lecturer, was born in Scotland in 1931. He lived and worked in Canada for many years, and in 1973 began lecturing at universities and health clinics in that country and throughout the United States.

Mr. Banks' unique philosophy and perceptions have provided new insights in the field of psychology and education. By applying this profound understanding to their respective fields, a growing number of teachers, doctors, and health-care and business professionals have experienced significant results in their work and their lives.

Sydney Banks is the author of such loved books as *Dear Liza,* *The Enlightened Gardener* and *The Enlightened Gardener Revisited.*

———➤●◄———

The Missing Link

Contents

Foreword

The author's gift and the greatest contribution of this book is the ability to unify the fields of psychology and spirituality.

This book, *The Missing Link*, connects the spiritual nature and the psychological nature of humanity. It shows the reader that these facets of life are, and always have been, *one* – just as seven days and one week are two different terms denoting the same unit of time.

The Missing Link

The author's words attempt to show us that all fields of knowledge are like the hues of the rainbow behind a prism; they only *appear* to be different from the light on the other side.

I recommend this book to anyone, professional, student or layman, who is looking for a deep, interesting, psychological or philosophical journey that will stimulate the mind and give the reader food for thought.

George Pransky, PhD, MFCC

Preface

The truth in this book speaks directly to the heart and soul of the reader. It opens the door to an inner life of stability and contentment which everyone intuitively knows, yet many have lost sight of in their daily pursuits. In the loving voice of an author who speaks from the certainty of enlightenment, this book offers solace to the world-weary, hope to the discouraged, direction to the lost and contentment to the discontented.

The Missing Link

It speaks simply, yet with
profound wisdom, of the inborn
potential for the well-being,
peace and happiness of all
mankind which is accessible and
near at hand. It illuminates the
power of the human spirit in a
way that transcends differences
and evokes the best in all people.
No one can read this book
without being touched and
inspired.

Judith A. Sedgeman, Ed. D.

Introduction

There are those in this world
who believe miracles do not
happen. I can assure such skeptics
that they do.

With hope and faith as beacons,
anything can happen.

*If these writings bring a second
chance of life to just one human
being, my work has not been in vain.*

Sydney Banks
March 1998

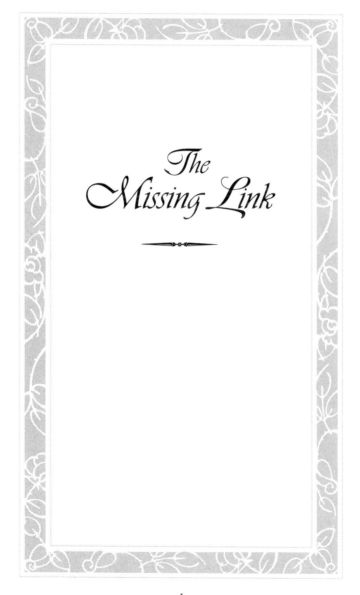

The
Missing Link

The Missing Link

*O*ne of the greatest misconceptions ever is the belief that...

"It takes years to find wisdom."

Many experience time, few experience wisdom.

The achievement of mental stability and peace of mind is *one* thought away from everyone on earth... *if* you can find that one *thought.*

Throughout time, human beings have experienced insights that spontaneously and completely changed their behavior and their lives, bringing them happiness they previously had thought impossible.

Finding wisdom has nothing to do with time.

Achieving mental stability is a matter of finding healthy *thoughts* from moment to moment. Such *thoughts* can be light years or a second away.

The spiritual energy of all things, whether in form or formless, is known by many names.

Nature is the physical form the spiritual energy has taken.

Believe me, the subtle truth all people seek will never be found in the illusion of form called nature.

Look deep inside your soul; this is where you will find the answer.

Your thoughts and feelings are a mirror of your soul.

Each living soul experiences life as an individual. This is why all humans live and see a separate reality.

The divine truth that lies within each living soul never changes. It is eternal.

The divine passes from the formless to form, and as human beings we are both spectators and participants in this spiritual theater called life.

The great mystics of the world
who tried to explain such
knowledge had no choice but to
speak in metaphors, knowing
their words were only a
representation of the spiritual
wisdom that lies within the
consciousness of *all* human
beings.

All human psyches are rooted in
universal truth and no person's
psyche is better than any other's.
Only to the degree of the individual's
psychological and spiritual
understanding does it appear
to vary.

Words are merely a form. Listen not to words, but to *that which words attempt to convey.*

Remember… *it is not the clay that represents the sculpture, but the form the artist has molded it into.*

Just like the clay of the sculpture, *thought* is not reality. However, our personal realities are molded via our thoughts.

The Missing Link

At the moment of birth, the
virgin mind discovers *creation*,
and the duality of life is born.
Henceforth you live in a world
governed by *thought*.

When clarity and purity of
thought are present, the answer
you seek will present itself, for
what you seek is with you and
has been with you always.

In the silence of our minds lies
creative incubation, bringing the
wisdom and the joy we all seek.

The
Theosopher

The Theosopher

*P*hilosophers search for basic principles. They gain knowledge by reading books and studying other people's opinions and concepts, then mold them together with their own personal opinions of life.

A theosopher's understanding comes from a direct experience using his or her own *innate* knowledge, or if you wish, from what is sometimes known as *Original Thought.*

Philosophy examines the known physical world. Theosophy hosts both the world of form and the formless.

To seek truth from the form alone is only half the truth; it traps you in a cosmic lie.

Everyone on earth is both a philosopher and a theosopher.

One is a learned intellectual process. The other is a realization of knowledge from within the depths of our own consciousness.

The Missing Link

Such knowledge cannot be
bought or sold like a commodity
in the marketplace, nor is it found
in some far-off land.

It is hidden in the depths of
your soul.

This is why such knowledge can
only be found through an insight
from one's *own* inner wisdom.

The Missing Link

————➤◆◄————

Everyone in this world shares
the same innate source of
wisdom, but it is hidden by the
tangle of our own misguided
personal thoughts.

Three Principles

Three Principles

Mind, Consciousness and *Thought* are the three principles that enable us to acknowledge and respond to existence.

They are the basic building blocks, and it is through these three components that all psychological mysteries are unfolded.

They are what I call the psychological trinity.

Mind, Consciousness and *Thought* are spiritual gifts that enable us to see creation and guide us through life.

All three are universal constants that can never change and never be separated.

All philosophies are born via these three gifts and are a direct result of the correct or incorrect usage of these same principles.

All psychological functions are born from these three principles.

The Missing Link

All human behavior and
social structures on earth are
formed via *Mind, Consciousness*
and *Thought.*

In chemistry two or more
elements create compounds. It is
the same with the psychological
elements… *Mind, Consciousness*
and *Thought.* These three
elements create psychological
compounds that are our own
personal psychological realities.

Healthy compounds – feelings,
such as compassion, humility,
love, joy, happiness and
contentment – are all rooted
in *positive* thoughts.

Hate, jealousy, insecurity, phobias
and feelings of depression are all
compounds of *negative* thoughts.

The Missing Link

All feelings derive and become
alive, whether negative or
positive, from the power of
Thought.

No matter what you *think* about,
it has to be a compound. Even if
you disagree with what I say, it's
your *thought.*

All three elements – *Mind,*
Consciousness and *Thought* – are
the lifeline to our very existence.
It is through these three elements
that we have the power to realize
the very existence of life.

Mental functioning cannot
possibly exist without the three
psychological elements. They are
the building blocks of all mental
behavior.

There are no more, nor any less,
than these three. They create all
human experience.

The Missing Link

Mind, *Consciousness* and
Thought are the complete
Trinity of all psychological
functioning. Without one the
others are non-existent.

All living creatures, great or
small, interpret what they
think of life via these three
divine gifts.

Mind

Mind

Every human mind has direct access to its experience here on earth, and the human mind always has access to its own spiritual roots... from whence it came.

The *Universal Mind,* or the *impersonal mind,* is constant and unchangeable.

The *personal mind* is in a perpetual state of change.

All humans have the inner ability to synchronize their *personal mind* with their *impersonal mind* to bring harmony into their lives.

The Missing Link

Some believe the brain and the mind are the same. But there has to be a power behind the brain to make it function.

The brain and the mind are two entirely different things.

The brain is *biological.*
The mind is *spiritual.*

The brain acts like a computer: whatever you put into it is all you get out. This is *logic.*

The Missing Link

An important thing to realize
is that *Universal Mind* and
personal mind are *not* two minds
thinking differently, but two
ways of using the same mind.

The Missing Link

The world in the form of nature is a *reflection* of the human mind, which creates an *illusionary gap* between the spiritual and the physical.

This gap, in turn, creates the *duality of life.* Trapped in this duality, our minds become full of disillusionment and lostness.

As the human mind ascends in divine consciousness, the gap between subject and object begins to vanish and the oneness of life emerges.

The Missing Link

There is one *Universal Mind*,
common to all, and wherever you
are, it is with you, always.

There is no end or limitation,
nor are there boundaries, to the
human mind.

Consciousness

Consciousness

All living creatures were given the power of *Mind*, *Consciousness* and *Thought*, which enables them to observe divine creation, or form.

Consciousness is the gift of awareness.

Consciousness allows the recognition of form, form being the expression of *Thought*.

The Missing Link

Somewhere in the innermost
recesses of our consciousness lie
the answers to the questions all
mankind seeks.

As our consciousness descends,
we lose our feelings of love and
understanding, and experience
a world of emptiness,
bewilderment and despair.

As our consciousness ascends, we
regain purity of *Thought* and, in
turn, regain our feelings of love
and understanding.

The Missing Link

Mental health lies within the consciousness of all human beings, but it is shrouded and held prisoner by our own erroneous thoughts.

This is why we must look past our contaminated thoughts to find the purity and wisdom that lies inside our own consciousness.

When the wise tell us to look *within,* they are directing us beyond intellectual analysis of personal thought, to a higher order of knowledge called *wisdom.*

Wisdom is an innate intelligence
everyone possesses deep
within their souls, before the
contamination of the outer world
of creation.

Find the spiritual wisdom that
will guide you through life from
within.

This is where you will find the
feelings of love, understanding
and contentment.

The Missing Link

That the deaf man cannot hear
the sound of the crashing ocean
waves, or the blind man cannot
see the beauty of an autumn sky,
does not mean the sea and the
sky do not exist.

So, like the blind man, close
your eyes.

Like the deaf man, block your
ears; go inside and realize…that
which you seek has been there,
within you, all along.

This is when the blind will see
and the deaf will hear.

Thought

Thought

Thought is a divine tool, nothing more, nothing less, only a tool. A wise person, like a good tradesman, uses this tool to the best of his or her ability.

The power of *Thought* is not self-created.

Thought is a divine gift, which serves you immediately after you are born.

Thought is the creative agent we use to direct us through life.

Thought is the master key that opens the world of reality to all living creatures.

Thought is the missing link that gives us the power to recognize the illusionary separation between the spiritual world and the world of form.

The Missing Link

Thought on its own is a
completely neutral gift.

Thought is not reality; yet it is
through Thought that our realities
are created.

It is what we as humans put into
our thoughts, that dictates what
we think of life.

The Missing Link

Among the greatest gifts given to us are the powers of free thought and free will, which give us the stamp of individuality, enabling us to see life as we wish.

These same gifts can also be the greatest weaknesses of humanity. We often lack the strength to change our minds, so we get stuck in the negative thoughts and behaviors of the past.

The purer your thoughts are, the more love and understanding will be in your heart.

Positive thoughts create a healthy mind and a stable life.

Optimism is a spiritual quality and a guiding light that will lead you to your happiness.

Pessimism, on the other hand, is a disease of the human thought system that leads the thinker into the darkness of despair.

Negative thoughts create negative feelings, which in turn create negative behaviors and are the seeds of human suffering.

"As you sow, so shall ye reap."

The Missing Link

When our minds are in unity
with that which is good, then our
thoughts no longer hold us
prisoner to that which is evil.

When you start to see the power
of *Thought* and its relationship to
your way of observing life, you
will better understand yourself
and the world in which you live.

To find that which you seek,
discard all thought that there is
a separation between the *spiritual*
and the *physical* world.

The Missing Link

The wise medicine men in the
Native North American culture
spoke of the world as *one* spirit,
referring to the creator of all
things as the *"Great Spirit."*

This was their way of explaining
the oneness of life.

Thought is a divine tool that is
the link between you and your
divine inheritance, and is at the
core of all psychological
functioning.

You can't even be aware of
creation without the presence
of *Thought*.

Thought is the missing link
between mental sickness and
mental health. *Thought* is also the
missing link between happiness
and sadness.

Your *personal mind* activates
your thoughts and makes them
good or bad.

You have no control over what
others think, but you do have the
power to control what you think.

The Missing Link

Our thoughts are the camera, our eyes are the lens. Put them together and the picture we see is reality.

In the silence beyond all things lies the divine knowledge that will help guide you through life.

Look *within your own consciousness,* for here lies the answer to all of humanity's problems.

The Missing Link

Your thoughts are like the artist's
brush. They create a *personal*
picture of the reality you live in.

Thought, like the rudder of a ship,
steers us to the safety of open
waters or to the doom of rocky
shores.

The wise man says,
"I think, therefore, I am."

The fool says,
"I don't *think* so."

The Missing Link

People often speculate how many components there are to thought.

There are no components to thought. *Thought* is a divine power. It is an element that can never be broken down into smaller segments.

It is we human beings that use *Thought* to produce such things as our feelings, moods and our overall perceptions of life.

Thought can be used in an *infinite* number of ways.

The more we dwell on the positive side of life, the more *hope* becomes a beacon, attracting positivity into our lives and guiding us to a steadfast and more contented way of life.

Many people make the mistake of believing that their moods create their thoughts; in reality, it is their thoughts that produce their moods.

The *personal mind* is the creator of all activity. The *personal mind* is the creator of all misery, all expectations, all ideas and all false deities.

The Missing Link

Hope and faith go together. With
hope and faith in your heart, you
will find the perfect path you
seek.

The Missing Link

When the desires of your mind
trouble your spirit, your life
becomes turmoil. My advice is to
learn to free yourself from too
many desires.

Life on earth is short, so beware
of striving for fame and fortune.
Many who find them never live
to enjoy them.

The Missing Link

Many people would succeed in
life if their ambitions weren't so
above their abilities.

Many who strive for the moon
begin their journey by tripping
over their own feet.

Everything on earth comes from one divine source. Our personal thoughts determine what we think of the form it has taken in our lives.

Thought is related to our five senses.

Our senses have no ability to discriminate. They are controlled and informed by our personal power of *Thought*. Without *Thought*, our five senses would be of no value.

The Missing Link

Our five senses and our egos
are but particles of the whole, just
as the illusion of time and space
are only particles of the whole.

The answer people seek lies not
in their separate beliefs, but in the
realization that *Thought* is the
common denominator in all
psychological and spiritual
understanding.

The Duality of Life

The Duality of Life

Nature is a cosmic illusion suspended within the boundaries of time, space and matter.

When one awakens from this illusionary dream state, it is known as the *Great Awakening.*

When people search for truth, they often look in two directions – at the form and at the formless – creating the idea of a duality in life.

The Missing Link

The life force beyond all
things has no form, yet it gives
form to all things.

The Missing Link

In the illusory world of thought, many believe the *inner self* is God and the *outer self* is the body. But I can assure you, the inner self and the outer self are the same thing.

Your eyes must see in the singular if you want to find truth.

When you understand this, you will see through the illusionary duality of life.

All life is divine energy,
whether in form or formless.

When this energy takes form,
we call it nature.

Both the form and the
formless together create the
whole, the *oneness* of life, that
which we call God.

Nothing can possibly be greater
or separate from the whole. Only
the ego suffers such delusions.

Our *personal mind*, or what
is sometimes referred to as the
ego, galvanized with our
consciousness, equals our reality
in its entirety.

Our ego, combined with our five
senses, often creates distorting
lenses that stop us from evolving
to our true spiritual nature.

At times we are captivated by our own ego and become prisoners of our contaminated thoughts.

Ego creates self-importance and is strictly related to the personal self and the personal intellect.

The ego creates duality and separates us from the great divine oneness and the wisdom we seek.

The Missing Link

Do not try to understand the words of the wise from an intellectual perspective.

Listen for a positive *feeling.*

Positive feelings will bring you the answer you seek. Delving into the workings of your ego won't.

The Missing Link

Do not ponder on the subject of ego. If you do, your labor will be in vain.

Focus on the *missing link* between our psychological nature and our spiritual nature.

The truth you seek does not come from books or the spoken word, but from within the soul of humanity.

The Missing Link

Nothing on earth can be more paradoxical than truth, for truth represents both the form and the formless.

Without one, the other is only half the puzzle.

Without one, the other is of little value and is a cosmic lie.

The Missing Link

As we start to regain the
true relationship between our
personal intelligence and the
spiritual wisdom that lies within,
we develop a higher degree of
intelligence and common sense.
This, in turn, clears up our
misguided lives.

Seeking Enlightenment

Seeking Enlightenment

We all seek enlightenment whether we are aware of this fact or not, and my friend, I tell you this…

Purer thoughts are the rungs of the ladder that lead to success.

The Universal center of all things, we call God.

The individual center, we call a soul.

The Missing Link

In the depth of our souls, we
discover our divine inheritance.

It is not the power of the word or the
determination of our might, but the
deep and silent workings of our
minds which bring the inner self
and the outer self *together, into*
harmony.

This is why many try to silence
their minds through meditative
contemplation. They seek a purer
state of *Thought.*

The Missing Link

My words may seem too
simple, but I say again, the truth
is simple.

Look for common sense; plain,
old-fashioned common sense.

When seeking wisdom, one is
very apt to find that in simplicity
lies complexity. Those who don't
realize the profound nature of
such simplicity are very apt to
expound on their findings,
losing the essence.

The Missing Link

Look for psychological *logic…*
the logic of the psyche.

Before the formation of physical
reality and the contamination of
personal thought, *soul* and
consciousness were the same
divine intelligence.

The Missing Link

Cut off from innate wisdom, a
lost thinker experiences isolation,
fear and confusion.

This is why there are so many
horrible atrocities throughout the
world. Newspapers are full of
wars, killings, children starving.

Ignorance of our own inner
wisdom is the cause of sin. There
would be no sin without such
ignorance.

The malfunction of our own personal thought system instigates the breakdown of personal relationships and leads to the crumbling of societies, causing unnecessary suffering and sadness.

The misled *thoughts* of humanity, alienated from their inner wisdom, cause all violence, cruelty and savagery in this world.

Since the beginning, the state of any society is a direct result of its conditioned way of thinking.

The Missing Link

As you think, so you shall hear.

The sage hears fools
and wise alike.

The fool hears only fools.

Selecting a Teacher

Selecting a Teacher

There are so many teachers in the world and so many theories about life. When selecting a teacher, ask yourself…

Is my teacher a well-balanced person?

Is she or he happy?

Does my teacher reflect and demonstrate the quality of life I desire?

If the answer to any of these questions is no, move on in your journey. Otherwise you may become one of the blind, led by the blind.

The Missing Link

I have great admiration for the clergy and therapists of this world. They are both helpers of humanity; only their approach and words differ.

The preacher attempts to purify our souls.

The therapist attempts to purify our consciousness.

The Missing Link

Originally, psychology examined the connection between *mind* and *soul*, until that theory was abandoned.

When psychologists stopped investigating the connection between *mind* and *soul*, they lost two of the most important clues to what they sought.

They focused instead on behavior, leading us away from our true psychological nature, ultimately encouraging us as passive victims of life.

From behaviorism a multitude of techniques arose. But I can assure you, techniques are to therapists as rituals are to the church. They lead you away from the very truth you seek.

Please realize, I am not condemning current teachings. I am simply saying that many don't realize the importance of finding one's *own* inner wisdom.

There is an enormous difference between finding your *own* inner wisdom and adopting someone else's beliefs.

The Missing Link

If you take on someone else's belief to replace a belief of your own, you may experience a temporary placebo effect, but you have not found a lasting answer. However, if you replace an old belief with a realization from *your* own inner wisdom, the effect and results are superior and permanent.

It is one thing to *listen* to the words of the wise and quite another to be a *follower.*

Any good teacher will tell you never to be a follower. A wise teacher will draw out your innate knowledge.

The Missing Link

Followers fail. They readily adopt another's beliefs and cease to think for themselves.

Never follow the words of others blindly, or you will only take on another person's reality. You will only hinder your progress by seeking fool's gold.

Use your own common sense.

The Missing Link

Beware of cults and organizations
that want to strip you of your right
to think freely.

If you become a *follower*, you lose
your independence and become a
slave to someone else's ideas and
beliefs; you give up your *free
will* and *freedom of thought*, two
extremely valuable assets in life.

Living in the Now

Living in the Now

Through the centuries, the wise have told us to live in the *now*. This is why I say to you…

The past is a ghost that cannot be held in the palm of your hand.

The future cannot be grasped, no matter how desirable or enticing it may appear.

Nor can the present be held, no matter how beautiful or exciting.

The Missing Link

Begin the process of nourishing
the soul by living in the *now*.

Forget the past and the future,
and *just be*, and you will surely be
rewarded by living in the *now*.

When Eastern mystics describe
the *now*, they are not talking
about today as a specific day of
the month and year. Their
meaning goes deeper. When such
people refer to the *now*, they
mean the *personal mind* is free
from the contaminants of
yesterday's memories and fears.

The Missing Link

This in turn frees the mind to see with clarity things as they *are*, not through distorted memories and apprehensions.

Living in the *now* requires a clear mind.

In clearing our minds, we may have to give up something to receive something.

If you wanted to replace a glass of stale wine with fresh wine, first you must pour out the old wine. It is the same with clearing our minds of unwanted, stale thoughts.

The Missing Link

We must rid ourselves of yesterday's negative thoughts to receive today's new and positive feelings.

I do not ask anyone to ignore their past experiences. This would be denial, and denial is *not* a healthy state.

Instead, seek a clearer understanding of the past; realize that the negative feelings and emotions from past traumatic experiences are *no longer* true. They are merely memories, a collection of old, stale thoughts.

The Missing Link

As surely as rust slowly destroys the strongest steel, hate and negative thoughts erode the soul of humanity.

Negative thoughts are like scratches on a window: they stop you from seeing life with clarity. When the negative thoughts cease, the scratches disappear and the window becomes crystal clear. Then the beauty and positive aspects of life can be seen.

The past is dead. Forget what is old and dead, and start life anew.

Discard the restless, haunting
ghosts of yesterday and set
yourself free to live the beauty
of today.

Change the pattern of
your thoughts from negative
to positive; automatically the
condition of your life will change
for the better.

The Missing Link

Just as the gardener rids a
garden of unwanted weeds, we
must rid our minds of
pernicious thoughts, which
like weeds crowd out the
beauty from our minds.

I call the process of casting
away negative thoughts a
spiritual mind treatment.

Our *thoughts* are our guide;
a good guide navigates
through the maze of life by
following the pathway of *love*
and *understanding.*

The Missing Link

If your thoughts wander onto a negative and rocky path, don't take them too seriously.

Refrain from analyzing, because, I guarantee you, you will analyze yourself forever, never reaching an end, and fail bitterly to find peace of mind.

What happened in the past may have influenced our present-day personal or social problems, but please believe me, there is no answer to these problems in the past. Only in the now can the answer be found.

The Missing Link

The intensity and importance of
such events dissipates as we see
that the past is *no longer a reality,*
but a *memory* carried through
time via our *own* thoughts.

Deal not with conditions of the
past, but look to the laws of cause
and effect. See the effect and
consequences *thought* has on
our everyday lives.

Seek simplicity and logic...
psycho-*logic.*

When your mind is full of
negative thoughts, you
automatically see and live
in a negative reality.

By the same rule, a mind
centered on positive thoughts
automatically lives in a far more
pleasant reality.

Let your negative thoughts go.
They are nothing more than
passing thoughts. You are then on
your way to finding the *peace of
mind* you seek, having healthier
feelings for yourself and for
others.

This is simple logic.

Feelings

Feelings

*O*ur *feelings* are the barometer of our *thoughts*.

When the mind is filled
with positive thoughts, cause and
effect rule, resulting in a positive
feeling.

When the mind is filled
with negative thoughts, again
cause and effect rule, creating a
negative *feeling*.

Our *feelings* are evidence of our mental well-being. Find positive and loving *feelings,* for they will guide you through life far better than resentment and grudges.

Positive thoughts and feelings will assist you to discover the mental health and wisdom that lie within you.

When you learn to forgive those who have wronged you in the past, you clear your mind and bring harmony into your life, allowing you to see what *is,* instead of what *isn't.*

The Missing Link

What isn't... *is life seen through distorted memories.*

What is... *is life seen as it truly is now, clear of all falsehoods.*

The tormented mind, which entertains love and forgiveness as guests, will surely attain new heights.

Love &
Forgiveness

Love & Forgiveness

*L*ove and *understanding*
harmonize the mind of humanity
to its true inner nature.

*What you give in life is what
you receive.*

To give love is to receive love.

A mind full of love and good
feelings can never go wrong.

Love and *forgiveness* go hand-
in-hand. Without them, life is
encumbered by ill feelings and
unhappiness.

The Missing Link

Judging your own faults or
the faults of others leads to
unhappiness. A mind that dwells
in non-judgment is a contented
mind.

A heart full of love is void of
all judgment and is filled with
divine spirit.

My love is like a red, red rose;
Its fragrance fills the air;
It guides me to a place of light,
Instead of dark despair.

The Missing Link

Forgiveness is divine, and has
wonderful effects on our lives.

Forgiveness is a powerful remedy
to clear thoughts of negative
memories. It frees us from the
emotional prisons of our past,
providing opportunities to start
life anew.

Forgiveness brings forth peace of
mind. Without forgiveness, the
road through life is paved with
doubt and misery.

An unforgiving mind burdens
one with negative thoughts,
holding onto yesterday's hurts. It
contaminates and prevents the
thinker from living a happy
life *now.*

It is forgiveness that allows you
to see today as a new experience.

God has already forgiven you
for yesterday's mistakes, so why
don't you forgive yourself?

To dwell on past trials and
tribulations is to *deny* the
moment.

The Missing Link

If you live in the past, you can never find happiness. *You are trying to live in a reality that no longer exists.*

It is a misconception to think that if you forgive someone who has harmed you, you are somehow condoning their behavior, making yourself vulnerable so that you will allow them to repeat their hurtful action.

This is not so. There is a vast difference between forgiving a *person* and forgiving an *act*.

The Missing Link

For example, say you were at the zoo and you approached a tiger's cage. If you were silly enough to put your hand through the bars and the tiger, being a tiger, ripped your hand open, you would probably have cursed the tiger. Later on, though, as you thought about it, you'd realize it really wasn't the tiger's fault. You would forgive the tiger. Yet you undoubtedly would have learned not to stick your hand into the cage again.

The Missing Link

Forgiveness releases *you* from mental anguish and pain, and all the horrible negative feelings an *unforgiving mind* experiences.

When you learn to *forgive,* you see with clarity the ignorance and the innocence of those who trespass against you.

You realize that hanging onto old grudges is like a miser in deep water clutching at a bag of fool's gold, unaware that the fool's gold is just heavy, useless rocks weighing him down.

The Missing Link

There is no way to guarantee a trouble-free life.

Life is like any other contact sport. You may encounter hardships of one sort or another.

Wise people find happiness not in the absence of such hardships, but in their ability to understand them when they occur.

Wisdom

Wisdom

Spiritual Wisdom lies within the consciousness of all living creatures. It is formless. The second it is revealed to a human soul, it has taken on a form that can only represent its true nature.

In the old Hawaiian religion, the Kahunas or wise priests said the wisdom they were trying to convey was a secret that could not be told.

The Missing Link

They were not intentionally
withholding the secret, but
literally could not convey it by
words alone, words only being
symbolic of their true meaning.

The answer sought is *beyond
the word.*

No one can give away wisdom.
A teacher can only lead you to it
via words, hoping you will have
the courage to look *within yourself*
and find it inside your *own*
consciousness...

Beyond the word.

The Missing Link

The wisdom humanity seeks lies *within the consciousness* of all human beings, trapped and held prisoner by their own personal minds.

Wisdom is not found in the world of form, nor in remote corners of the globe. Wisdom lies *within our own consciousness.*

Only *you* have the golden key to your soul and the wisdom that lies within.

The Missing Link

Those who refuse good advice cannot be helped. Good advice is seldom welcomed in the mansion of a fool. Anyone who tries to force learning on such a person is indeed a fool as well.

To find wisdom, elevate your consciousness. Seek a *grateful feeling* for what you already have in life.

The Missing Link

Gratitude and satisfaction have wonderful effects on our souls. They open our minds, clearing the way for wisdom and contentment to enter.

Once you become grateful, the prison bars of your mind will fall away. Peace of mind and contentment will be yours.

The ego and our intellect are functions of our personal minds, whereas wisdom is a function of the spirit. One is mortal, the other immortal.

Intellectual observation is ego,
after form.

Wisdom is found before the
formation of form.

Ego is only what you *think* you
are and what you think of life,
nothing more, nothing less.

Our intellect and our inner
wisdom should work together to
create harmony in our lives.
However, if the intellect lacks
wisdom, chaos reigns. This is the
state of the world today.

The Missing Link

Those who have found a balance
between their intelligence and
their innate wisdom are the lucky
ones.

As human beings we must
look closely at the relationship
between our spiritual nature and
our psychological nature.

Here we will find the answers
we seek to change the deplorable
state of the world.

The Missing Link

The consciousness of humankind
must be elevated. Only then,
when the spiritual and physical
realities are united, will we find
the power and intelligence to
guide us through life.

Wisdom cleans the channels of
your mind and brings sanity into
your life.

You must find it for yourself.

Pure soul and pure consciousness
can only temporarily be separated
by the erroneous thoughts of
humanity because *soul* and
consciousness are one and the
same.

Wisdom is divine nourishment
for the soul; it is a God-given
intelligence before the
contamination of form or
personal thought.

The Missing Link

With wisdom people see *beyond* the filters and biases of race and culture, to realize the beauty in everyone.

Such understanding enables people to stop fearing and distrusting those who are different, to see the commonality of human beings regardless of cultural differences.

Wisdom applied to society would do more than anything else to halt the ethnic clashes and wars the world suffers from today.

Wisdom is impersonal.

Wisdom is immortal and unchangeable.

Wisdom is the path to all spiritual understanding.

Wisdom is also the path to all psychological understanding.

The Missing Link

Our psychological nature
and our spiritual nature are
entwined, and the more they are
harmonized, the more contented
we will be.

Wisdom brings *common sense to
those who find it.*

The Missing Link

The solutions to outwardly
complex problems created by
misguided thoughts will not arise
from complicated analytical
theory, but will emerge as an
insight, wrapped in a blanket of
simplicity.

Trying to deal with marital
problems, for example, using a
variety of methods and
techniques may meet with little
or no success. However, when a
lost couple finds *wisdom* and
understanding within their *own*
consciousness, their marital
problems will start to dissipate.

Seek without seeking, for
what you hope to attain is
already within you.

The Missing Link

That which you seek has no form.

If you attempt to put a shape
on the formless, you will never
find it.

Attempt to describe the formless
with words, and the word turns
the formless into form, creating
an illusion and leading you
further away from that which
you seek.

The Missing Link

———◆———

There are many ways to find the
inner wisdom that will lead you
to a healthier state of mind.

*You must exercise your
freedom of choice to decide on
your own individual path.*

No matter which path you take,
the wisdom you seek will always
be found within the depths of
your *own* consciousness.

The Missing Link

—————➤◆◄—————

Bless those who
have sinned against you,
For they have lost their way.
Reach out your hand
and help them
To live a happy day.

The End